Have You Ever Been Convicted of a Felony?

Get Hired Despite Having a Past Criminal Record

Shannon Ben Dailey

Have You Ever Been Convicted of a Felony?

Copyright © 2018 by Shannon Ben Dailey.

Printed in the United States of America. All rights reserved under International Copyright Law. Contents and/or cover may not be reproduced in whole or in part in any form without the express written consent of the Publisher.

ISBN-13: 978-1535399753

Printed in the United States of America.

www.LiveDailey.com

CONTENTS

Disclaimer	7
Introduction	9
Hustling Mentality	11
Know Thyself	15
Completing an Employment Application	21
The Big Question	25
What Are You Wearing?	33
My Hair Promotion	37
Body Art	41
The Interview	45
Conducting an Interview	51
Challenge Questions	55
Guard at the Gate	59
Do Your Research	63
It Is What It Is	67
Reliable Transportation	71

Disclaimer

All opinions expressed by the author in this book are solely the author's opinions and do not reflect the opinions of companies he has worked for and/or consulted with, past or present. All suggestions and opinions mentioned are not guaranteed to work. Each suggestion and opinion in this book that may have been advised, applied, and implemented may produce different results based on your past convictions and work history. The author's opinions are based upon information he considers reliable, useful, and resourceful. Neither the companies mentioned nor the companies the author worked for in the past, presently works for, and/or consults with, along with any affiliates and/or subsidiaries, warrant this book's completeness or accuracy, and it should not be relied upon as such. The author and/or his affiliates and/or subsidiaries are not under any obligation to update or correct any information provided in this book.

Introduction

My name is Shannon Dailey, and I am an African-American male and a former convicted felon, born and raised in Cleveland, Ohio. I wrote a book, *Dirt Road to Smooth Pavement*, which outlines my double conviction for drug trafficking and a weapons charge. I tell the story of how my life changed dramatically from making poor choices in my teen years as a drug dealer, with limited work history; to leaving the street behind; sharing my experience as a former felon; to getting hired for full-time positions within fortune 500 companies. I went from temp jobs to permanent positions; to getting hired directly into management, a vice president of sales and marketing position; to owning my own business; to doing what I am ultimately passionate about—helping others like me succeed.

Hustling Mentality

Terms like "do what I gotta do" or "whatever it takes" can put you in a position for failure. These type of statements come from what I call a "hustling mentality." A hustling mentality focuses on selfishness and greed. You want to make money so bad that you will do anything, which causes you to sacrifice your family, friends, and responsibilities just to make money. This mentality is not being a team player either. Often, you'll find yourself in conflict with co-workers and management. Doing what you gotta do will put you in a position to cut corners and lie to your peers. And when you finally get your paycheck, you'll be either too tired or too stressed out to enjoy it, or you will end up spending your money on "stuff," rather than on your responsibilities. The hustling mentality is never satisfied, nor do you live in peace or enjoy life—because you're too busy being busy. And because you're so busy, you tend to not take care of yourself by eating poorly, developing bad sleeping habits, and lacking exercise.

Just so we are clear, a hustling mentality is not the same as being hardworking. Hard workers focus on the task at hand. Hard workers set goals or have a vision, knowing that they will be rewarded with their paycheck. Their focus is on the business's needs and not just on their incomes. Because they know that they will be rewarded with their paycheck, they look for opportunities to grow in the company by way of promotion or a different position that comes with a greater reward, more income, and perks. Hard workers focus on completing the job they are assigned to do. So be a hard worker, not a hustler.

Here's another pet peeve. If I were to ask you what type of work you want to do, and your reply was, "Whatever is available or anything"—this is what you are really saying: "I'm just trying to get paid. It's all about me and my wants. I don't have a plan for my future. I don't care about your company. I am only in it for the money." In other words, you have a hustling mentality. Keep in mind no employer is hiring desperate people; they are hiring individuals that they feel are most qualified or willing to do the job. Hopefully, this paints a clearer picture of the hustling mentality. Now that we know that you are willing to work, do not apply for "any" job.

In my experience and the experience of other individuals in various professional fields, knowing what job to apply for and what companies are hiring ex-offenders is extremely important. I have spent many years applying for the wrong jobs, not because I was not qualified or did not want to do the work, but based on my past convictions. There are industries such as banking, financial institutions, some retailers (selling jewelry or other high-end products), or certain medical jobs that I need to avoid because, generally, they do not hire individuals with a criminal background. Certain retail positions, such as cashiering, may be hard to get hired for because you are applying for a job that either handles money or secured information, such as credit cards or personal information. When applying for work, it is very helpful to know where to apply for work and what companies hire ex-offenders.

There are several websites out there that offer additional tips and suggestions, along with companies that are hiring ex-offenders. Take time to find out who they are before applying for work. This way, you will be able to determine if you would be a good fit for that company; and if they offer a position, you can commit yourself to doing it.

Know Thyself

Hopefully, you have figured out where you want to work and what companies are hiring based on your former convictions. My question for you is, "Do you know what your natural abilities are?" Everyone has a talent or abilities of some type—whether you work well with your hands; are able to manage people, product, tasks, or situations; have an eye for detail; you're good at explaining things; or are simply a clean freak. There is something about you that comes naturally to you. Once you discover what that is, pursue it! When I was a drug dealer many years ago, I had several guys working under me. For lack of a better term, I was their manager or boss. Now, at the time, I had no idea that I was managing people and products, recruiting, training, and operating a business, just like any other legitimate business. Even though what I was doing was illegal, the concept of managing came naturally to me.

When I was first hired as a full-time employee, it was not a management position. In fact, I was working at a job I did not like, for a company I did not know anything about, and I had zero experience for the position I was hired for. My focus was to make some money, and I did for a short period of time. When it came to promotion time, I didn't get what I wanted (which was more money) because my focus was solely on money, so much so that I literally sucked at the work I was doing; and, therefore, I quit.

Then I went to a temporary agency, and the coordinator at the agency opened up my eyes to see my natural abilities by having me take a personality profile test. This test (which can be found online and at public libraries) helped me to see what type of person I am and what I am able to do effortlessly. That's when I saw that I am a problem solver, I am not afraid to lead people, come up with ideas to improve work flow, and help and talk to people. The temporary agency put me on an assignment working in the collections department of a very large corporation. This temp job became permanent, and the permanent job was my introduction to my career in management.

I had never done collections before, but after doing some research, I found the company to be interesting; and, therefore, I was willing to learn how to be a debt collector. With my willingness to learn, coupled with my natural abilities to be a problem solver and a good communicator, I became very good at collections. Though my goal was to be good at collections in the short term, I was determined to do more and to be more than a collector. This all happened when I shifted my focus from making money to using my natural abilities in this collection position, which made me one of the top collectors in that office, followed by promotions (more money), to, eventually, a career position in management.

So no matter if you're working at a fast food restaurant, convenience store, or cleaning toilets, remind yourself in that position, "This is a stepping stone to something greater." While you are in that position, work with excellence, and make sure the job you choose lines up with your natural abilities.

Have you ever frequented a store and the cashier was rude and unpleasant? Or been at a restaurant, and it looked like someone just threw the food on a plate? These are common examples of people doing a job that they do not want to do or don't have the natural talent to do. Therefore, they eventually become stressed; they develop an "I don't care" attitude; and before they know it, they'll either quit or get fired. I can't stress enough: Discover your abilities and talents, and apply for the position that would best suit your gifts—and watch your career and money grow.

Now, you may say, "I don't know what my natural abilities are." I would highly encourage you to take a personality profile test, which you can find online. If you take the test and are still having a challenge with discovering your abilities, focus on the job or position you would <u>like</u> to do. A lot of times, that job <u>you want or would like</u> to do is connected to your natural abilities.

Completing an Employment Application

The general rule is to use a black ink pen when completing employment applications. No red, pink with glitter in the ink, no felt tip, or calligraphy pens, please, just a simple black ballpoint pen. Blue is okay, but I highly suggest a black ballpoint pen. And never, ever complete an application in pencil. Believe it or not, ink colors and pencils shows signs of immaturity and lack of preparation on your part. When filling in the requested information, be as clear and as legible as possible. To accomplish this, I have a suggestion. Ready? Slow down. Take your time, relax. Breathe a little. You're not taking a test. You are not timed; it's an employment application. If you're a little nervous or lack confidence in the position you are applying for, it will show when completing your application.

Accuracy is more important than speed. Be sure to fill in every blank requested, including middle name or initial, your current address, prior employer's name, address, phone number, immediate supervisor or manager's name, hire and end dates, and wages. If you do not know this information from memory, be sure to have your resume with you (highly recommended), along with written details, including references, that may be requested on an employment application.

So, let's recap what you should have and know when completing an employment application:

- Black ballpoint pen

- Resume that includes the past three to four employers (names, addresses, phone numbers, and supervisors' names, start and end dates)

- Written detail of starting pay and ending pay for the last three to four employers, education information, job qualifications, and references

- Have your driver's license/state I.D., auto insurance card, social security card, and/or birth certificate

Even though this chapter is referring to completing a written application, you may be required to complete an employment application on a computer or online at the company or place of business. Be sure to have your resume, references, I.D., social security card, and/or birth certificate. If you are a foreign national, add passport and/or green card to the list of things you should have with you when completing an application at a company or place of business. I can't tell you how many times I've interviewed and hired individuals who only came in to complete an application and did not expect to be interviewed or even hired that same day. So, be prepared.

The Big Question

Nowadays, more and more employers have removed the big question, "Have you ever been convicted of a felon?" from their applications. Even if the question is not asked on paper, it may be asked during the interview. In the event you apply for employment where this question is still asked on the application, my hope is the following will provide you some guidance and confidence to address the question on paper and in the interview. Even though a number of employers removed it from the application, they do have the right to ask, so please be prepared and apply the following suggestions, if asked verbally.

I remember how I felt when I first completed an employment application after my second felony conviction. I felt scared. I was scared because I wasn't sure how to answer if I had ever been convicted of a felony, or in my case, felonies. If I told the truth, they may not hire me. If I lied on the application and they found out, they would fire me. And if I simply avoided answering the question, I assumed they would know I was hiding something, and I would not get hired.

So here's what I've discovered over the years of being <u>denied</u> employment, to being hired as an employee, to being the hiring manager that hires employees. TELL THE TRUTH! When answering "YES" to being convicted of a felony, you will most likely need to explain what happened, *briefly,* on the application and possibly again during your interview. As a suggestion when it comes to explaining the conviction, *keep it simple and brief*. The truth of the matter is most employers, including companies I worked for, conduct a criminal, federal, and possibly a credit check, before you are considered for employment. Answering the question is about integrity. It's to determine whether you can be trusted, and if you've moved on from your past convictions. To avoid answering the question, or by writing on the application that you will explain in the interview, DOES NOT explain your conviction. In addition, because you did not answer the question by not explaining yourself in writing, you may have just eliminated your chances of being hired. Furthermore, by NOT answering the question, it also tells the hiring manager that you do not follow instructions and may have an issue with authority (supervisor or manager), or that you are hiding something. Amazing, right? Avoiding one simple question can say a lot about you and your chances of being hired.

If and when you are asked to explain your conviction, *be brief*. Provide the type of conviction along with when you were arrested. If you are asked to explain in detail, again answer the question honestly, stating the offense you were convicted for, and write *briefly* what happened and how you have moved on with your life. The following are some great examples that have helped me and many others gain employment.

1. I was convicted of a fourth degree felony, June, 2004, for possession of marijuana for personal use. I no longer experiment with drugs, and I welcome the opportunity to discuss my conviction and how I've changed during our interview.

2. Over a decade ago, I was convicted of a drug possession charge. I served 18 months on probation; and since then, I've turned my life around and regret ever experimenting with drugs.

3. Over one year ago, I was in a desperate place and was arrested and convicted of handling stolen property. I have since received the help needed to turn my life around and move forward.

4. I was convicted of a second degree felony 36 months ago and spent 2 years in a correctional facility, and I

used that time to reform my life to be a responsible citizen.

5. Over a year ago, I was convicted of inside trading; I was sentenced to 6 months of jail time. During that time, I received the help and support needed and have not participated, nor choose to participate, in those activities that led to my past conviction.

6. Twenty-four months ago, I was involved in a domestic dispute case, I was found guilty, I served my probation time, and received the help (or treatment) needed to move past my poor choices to being the renewed person that I am today.

7. Many years ago, I was in a desperate place and was arrested for writing bad checks. After serving one month of incarceration, I am no longer in that

desperate place and have become a better person in spite of my poor choices back then.

When asked to explain your conviction in detail, you determine <u>how much detail</u> you provide, but keep it simple, nothing lengthy, and no matter what, answer the question.

On the application, you may be asked to write when you were convicted of your crime. This is the date you were arrested, not sentenced. The goal is to make your conviction seem old. There can be months between the time you were arrested to the time you were sentenced. Doing this can help put distance from your past conviction. For example, if you were arrested 13 months ago (over a year ago), but were sentenced before a judge 10 months ago, "over a year ago when you were arrested," sounds much older than "10 months ago" (after being sentenced.)

Also, if you have had more than one conviction, on the application, list your most recent conviction, rather than writing about every arrest. The reason being, there may not be enough room to list all your convictions; and it is very likely the company you are applying for already pulled a background check to verify your past anyway. Therefore, if you write about your older conviction instead of your most recent and the hiring manager finds out, this could leave the impression that you're trying to hide your recent convictions, which may lead to you not getting an interview or being employed.

What Are You Wearing?

When completing an application at a company or when going to an interview, I always suggest wearing professional or business casual attire. Men, wear an oxford shirt (button-up shirt) and tie, which I suggest with slacks, not khakis, and definitely NO jeans, athletic gear, or shorts. A suit is nice but not necessary. Make sure you wear leather casual or dress shoes. Make sure your shoes are polished and/or cleaned. Don't wear athletic shoes, or shoes that look like sneakers, sandals, or flip-flops.

Ladies, wear a blouse with slacks or a skirt. No shorts, miniskirts, or bodysuits. Wearing a suit or dress is recommended. If wearing pants, be sure they are not skintight. No jeans, leggings, spandex, or short shorts. Make sure you button up your blouse, your underclothing cannot be seen through your blouse, and nothing is tight fitting or revealing. No sandals, flip-flops, sneakers, high heels, riding boots, or open-toed shoes. If wearing heels, they should be no higher than one inch or so.

Guys and gals, whatever you decide to wear, please, please, please make sure your clothes are ironed. Clothes should also be fitting, not sagging or skintight, with no snags, holes, or missing buttons, and stain free.

What I'm about to say next may offend you, and that's not my intention at all. Everything you do in this life is on purpose, whether you recognize it or not—from the colors you select to the style of clothes you choose to wear. Your appearance can show the hiring manager that you are prepared and confident, or it can show you like to cut corners, are lazy, and cheap. With that said, DO NOT wear hand-me-downs or secondhand clothes from thrift stores to your interview. That suit or dress was fly in the 90's, but those days are over. Please spend a few bucks to update your wardrobe. And if you have no choice except to purchase clothes from a thrift or pre-owned clothing store, inspect the clothes thoroughly, and make sure they are current fashion and not from a past era.

When choosing what to wear, I suggest wearing solid colors. Stay away from flashy or bright colors, risqué looking designs, and crazy-patterned clothing. And to go one step further, I suggest not to wear clothing that has a designer name, logo, slogan, pictures, or graphics plastered all over it. Keep it simple and neat. Besides, if you do not have a lot of clothes, it's less likely that they will notice you wore the same black pants with a different color shirt during your next interview or orientation.

My Hair Promotion

Years ago, I was hired by a national retail chain as an assistant store manager. When I was first hired on, I had a low-cut afro, nice, neat, and groomed. Months after being hired, I was promoted to store manager of a half a million-dollar store. My store and team were producing record-breaking numbers month after month. During this time, I decided to let my hair grow out and eventually had braids; then, I started to grow my hair into locs while I was the store manager of the half a million-dollar store.

My goal was to be a district manager for this national retail chain, which meant I would have to manage a million-dollar or larger store before taking on the role of district manager. Months after having my hair in locs, I was approached by another African-American male who was the regional manager of this retail chain at that time. During one of our weekly manager meetings, the regional manager pulled me aside to tell me his story about his hair promotion. Keep in mind while he is telling me this story, he is clean shaven, and his hair is low-cut and lined. The regional manager said he, too, had braids years ago, and couldn't understand why he couldn't get past the store manager level and break into upper management of this fortune 200 company. He said he was told by another African-American to cut his hair and watch his career blossom. My regional manager told me how offended he was by the comment of this other person and felt that was the most ridiculous thing he had ever heard.

He said months went by and still no promotion, in spite of the success he created for the district he worked in. My regional manager said to himself, "What would it hurt to cut it off?" Worst-case scenario, he could grow it back if he did not get the promotion. The regional manager went through with it. After cutting his hair, he said in a matter of months he was promoted from district manager to regional manager, and he went on to be the first African-American regional vice president of this national chain.

My point? Your appearance has a lot to do with getting hired and promoted. Your appearance can decide between whether you have a job or a career. Shortly after he told me this, I, too, decided to cut my hair. No sooner had I cut my hair than I was promoted to a multimillion-dollar store, then moved up to hiring manager for my district, then assistant district sales manager, and I knew I was on my way to district manager. Honestly, I can't say that cutting my hair was the reason for my promotion, along with hard work, but it did not hurt. After doing some additional research and talking to other career-driven individuals, I realized corporate America is a lot like the military. Every person in the military is groomed and uniformed as a sign of unity and commitment. In corporate

America, unless you're in the sports or the entertainment industry, it is no different.

What I just mentioned is what has personally happened in my life and the lives of others that have shared their stories.

So when applying for a job, just like the clothes you wear, as mentioned in the prior chapter, your hair may have a role to play in getting hired as well. In my opinion, ladies can get away with wearing locs, braids, and long hair as compared to men. So men, if you choose to keep your locs, braids, or long hair, make sure it's clean and groomed, with no wild hairstyles. Ladies, also be cautious of creative hairstyles and colors. Even though you may look cute, it could possibly limit your chances of getting hired or promoted.

Body Art

Like the clothes you wear or your hairstyle with bright neon colors, tattoos, earrings, and piercings could possibly hinder your chances of getting hired for certain jobs and positions. Once you are employed, the company you end up working for may request that your tattoos be covered by clothing or some type of sleeve or band. Do not be offended if you are asked to remove certain earrings or piercings upon getting hired on. In fact, I suggest that you remove piercings and cover up your tattoos prior to completing an employment application or interview.

Back in the day, shortly after my second felony conviction, I walked into a placement agency to apply for work. Even though I have body art, it was not visible, but what I did have were two huge gold hoop earrings, one in each ear, with a gold chain around my neck. The agency rep allowed me to complete an application. Shortly after I completed my application at the agency, I was told to contact them in a couple of days to see if there were any positions available. They never returned one single call from all the messages I left after I visited the agency.

After being ignored by this agency, I decided to go to another placement agency; and to my surprise, they were a little different. This agency offered typing classes, computer program sessions, and more. They mentored their candidates on appearance, they offered personality profile testing to assist with matching their candidates to suitable jobs, and offered pointers on what to do during the interview for a permanent position. The rep at this agency complimented me on my earrings, but told me they must go and the chain, too. They also told me to wear a button-up, collared shirt. Needless to say, I followed the rep's advice and I got the job.

After I began working for a major corporation and things were going along very well, I stopped wearing my earrings altogether, which was a personal choice. Putting the earrings in and out of my ears every day before and after work became a hassle, and I didn't value the earrings as that important anyway. However, I've worked with employers over the years who did not mind employees wearing earrings and piercings. Once I was promoted to management, my earrings and gold chain were things of the past.

As for the body art, because so many people are tatted up, companies are becoming more lenient of showing body art, depending on what the art is and/or says. However, depending on the position and line of work you do, do not be offended or surprised when they offer you the job and request that you wear long-sleeved shirts or a sleeve to cover up your body art year-round.

The Interview

If you put into practice everything you have read thus far, and you have been scheduled for an interview, don't mess it up by being late! If you are <u>on time</u> to your interview, then <u>you are late!</u> If you are 10-15 minutes early, then you are actually on time. As you wait in the foyer or lobby to meet with the hiring manager, relax; you jumped one of the hardest hurdles, which was getting to the interview. Interviews are conducted to simply validate the information on the employment application or resume, and to make sure you are a good fit for the job based on how you answer interview questions. The hiring manager's job is to hire good employees. One of the best ways for hiring managers to determine if you are a good employee is by asking questions about you and your goals. How you answer the interview questions will help the hiring manager determine if you are a good fit. If you answer interview questions defensively, if you tend to avoid answering questions altogether, talk in riddles, don't enunciate very clearly, or if you use a lot of hand gestures and so forth, these are telltale signs as to whether or not hiring managers should hire you.

Let's break down what the hiring manager may discover based on the examples I gave.

1. Answering questions defensively - Usually, this is a sign that you're hiding something, or you are fearful.

2. Tending to avoid answering questions altogether – You're uncomfortable answering honestly, or simply were not prepared to answer that line of questioning.

3. Talking in riddles – This is a sign of being nervous or hiding something.

4. Not enunciating – This goes back to being either nervous or uncomfortable with giving an honest answer.

5. Using a lot of hand gestures – It's simply a distraction and could show signs of being nervous.

If you notice, three out of five things a hiring manager may notice are based on nervousness. So again, relax; the hard part is behind you. The interview generally is a conversation about the position you are being considered for, and to go over information on your resume and application. The interview is to see if you are a good fit for the position you are applying for, or possibly another position that you may not even know about. Your role is to demonstrate that you are what they need. Now, during the interview, you may be asked about your convictions. Just like I discussed in the "The Big Question," keep it simple. DO NOT be lengthy or repeat what happened over and over again. Do not apologize multiple times about your past, get emotional, or beat yourself up over what happened during your interview. Focus on what's happening, not what happened.

Maintain eye contact; this is not the time to stare off into space. Stay in control, keep it simple, and for heaven's sake, relax! Remember, they already read about your conviction on the employment application, along with the background check, prior to your interview. There's nothing you're going to say that "should" surprise them. They are looking for confidence. They are looking for the present you and not the past you.

Speaking of confidence. Here are several NO-NOs during the interview:

1. Do not chew gum.

2. Do not say, "Umm," "okay," or smack your lips repeatedly.

3. Do not make a fist or clench your hands together.

4. Do not tap your feet.

5. Do not nervously bounce your knee.

6. No nervous twitching.

7. No sighing, heavy breathing, or panting.

8. No scratching your head or chest, or rubbing your neck.

9. Most importantly, and this is crucial, slow down! Speak at a normal pace, not fast and high-pitched.

Stay in control and relax. They are looking to hire someone, and it might as well be you.

Conducting an Interview

As mentioned before, relax. Keep your answers to interview questions simple and to the point. While you are answering the questions and making small talk, listen carefully; this is very important. In the interview, DO NOT tell the hiring manager what you think they want to hear because you think that will increase your odds of getting hired. Do not tell them what they want to HEAR; TELL THE TRUTH. If you don't know something about a question they asked you, you simply don't know. If you never did that type of work before, do not say, "Yes, I've done that before" because you think that's what they expect from you. It will be only a matter of time before they will find out the truth. What the hiring manager is trying to find out is: Can you be trusted? Are you willing to learn? Are you only in it for the money? Are you a long-term employee looking to grow?

Your mission during the interview is not to sound convincing by lying or selling them on the idea you're a good person. Your goal is to be true to yourself. What I mean by that is you are not ghetto, you are not a thug, or bougie. You were not created this way; these are attributes that you decided to make a part of your life. Being ghetto is a personal choice based on what you see, hear, and desire. You were not born ghetto, even if you live in one. Being ghetto, a thug, or bougie is a personal choice. So in the interview, make a choice to be your true self. Be polite, smile, make eye contact, and give a firm handshake. No dap, secret handshakes or nods, just a simple firm handshake. Also during the interview, no matter what, do not flirt, make sexual suggestions, or stare at the hiring manager's anatomy. You are there to interview for work, not to find your next boo.

When I was a hiring manager for various corporations, one of the absolutely worst things you could say was, "What's up, my brother?" or use any type of slang or phrase because I am an African-American. I could not stand it when someone would use a common ground as leverage to persuade me to offer them the job. Nationality, religion, places lived, etc. should never be referenced as a plea for employment, or leveraged to get the job because of your common interest.

There's nothing wrong with using common ground to make small talk, but keep it professional. Small talk is for our benefit, not the hiring managers. Small talk is a nice way to get you to relax and shift the focus off of you and onto the hiring manager. For example, if the hiring manager mentions that they are from Cleveland, you could say, "So, what part of Cleveland are you from?" Let the hiring manager respond. "And what brought you to Columbus?" Let the hiring manager respond. "Did you always want to be a hiring manager for _____ (company name)?" Let the hiring manager respond. Do you see what I just did? I took something we have in common, made it into small talk, and got the hiring manager to talk about themselves and the company I'm interviewing for—which leaves an impression with the hiring manager that you seem like you belong, and you are very interested in knowing more about the company and the people you will be working with. Again, small talk is for your benefit to relax and show confidence by getting the hiring manager to dialogue with you, even if you feel a little nervous.

Challenge Questions

During the interview you may be asked questions like:

- Tell me about the last time you helped someone.

- Tell me one of your strengths and a weakness about yourself.

- Sell me this pen.

Believe it or not, it's not about having the right or wrong answer. It's about answering the question and seeing how you handle pressure, whether you talk about yourself or sell an object. Also, when being asked these general questions, be honest. Keep it simple, short, and general. Do not reminisce over how you saved kittens in the tree. Remember, answer the question, stick to the point, and keep it simple. When talking, make eye contact; remember, easy on hand gestures;

and stay on target. This exercise is about self-control, not necessarily about having the right answer.

As much as I did not like selling the pen to the hiring manager, I realized something. If they asked me the sell question, it was because they liked what they heard from me thus far, and the sell question is usually a question asked to wrap up the interview. If I received positive feedback from the hiring manager on how I sold the pen, this was my little indicator that I was going to be offered the job. If they gave me pointers on what I could have said differently, that, too, was an indicator that they were going to offer me the job. If they asked me to sell something else, that meant I was not convincing enough, and they were giving me a second chance. If I responded well on the second try, and they provided positive feedback or pointers, there was a good chance I may be offered the job. However, if the hiring manager gave me a second chance and they didn't give a favorable response on how I sold the pen, there was a good chance that I was <u>not</u> getting the job.

Keep in mind everything I am stating here is not hiring or firing law; it's not etched in stone that you're guaranteed the job. The examples and advice is based on my personal experience and the experience of others. The hiring manager may not even ask these questions at all, or they may ask a different line of questions. However, the goal here is to bring awareness during the interview process so that you can be prepared.

Guard at the Gate

When going into a business to request an employment application, be careful because the very person handing you the employment application may very well be the person who interviews you. Even worse, if that's not the person who will interview you, the hiring manager who is doing your interview will probably ask that person (gatekeeper) who handed you an application their opinion about you. If you didn't leave a good impression because you said "Umm" a thousand times, or you did not look presentable, or you were on your cell phone when they handed you an application—you might have just gotten fired before you got hired.

A gatekeeper is someone who may be the first point of contact over the phone or in person. The gatekeeper could the receptionist, secretary, or an employee of that company. They tend to screen sales calls and people looking for employment.

They may not be paid to be gatekeepers, but they ultimately inherit that role, and seem to be very good at screening calls and people who are interested in "their" company.

From the time you walk into the building to request and receive an application until the time you complete the application, the gatekeeper may be keeping their eyes on you. And if you don't leave a good impression on the gatekeeper, the hiring manager will hear about it. If the gatekeeper did not report anything good, the hiring manager may then begin to scrutinize your application for errors, or not look at it at all.

So here's what I suggest—and I know when I say this, you may feel like you're being abandoned or put into the time-out corner. My suggestion is that before you go into that business to request an employment application, turn your cell phone <u>off</u>, not to vibrate mode. Turn it either to airport mode or completely off. Do not be on a call, texting, or on social media while requesting or completing an employment application.

When you turn in your application and you are asked to wait for the next step from the potential employer, DO NOT BE ON YOUR PHONE. Just sit there and wait patiently, or read a magazine or newspaper, if it is available in the lobby. If there is nothing to read or do while you wait, DO NOT BE ON YOUR PHONE! Here's why: Patiently waiting without using your cell phone shows confidence that you are ready to be interviewed and hired. Also, if you are asked to wait, chances are you are about to be interviewed on the spot. More and more businesses today are interviewing potential applicants on the spot or hiring the same day the application is completed, so be ready. Secondly, no one want to hear your conversation about how your dude Mookie was dumped by Peaches, because her girlfriend Kiki said she thought Mookie was cute.

Do Your Research

One of the worst things you can do is to know absolutely nothing about the company you want to work for. You need to know, beyond the hiring sign posted on the window, why are they hiring? How long have they been in business? How did they get started as a company? What is the company known for? Once you can answer these questions, the next set of questions you need to ask is: Where do I see myself in that company? How long do I want to work for that company, roughly? How will I make that company better?

Now, let's break down why you want to know those answers about the company.

1. <u>Why are they hiring?</u> Are they hiring because their success requires them to expand, and they need more quality workers to do so?

2. <u>How long have they been in business?</u> This is about longevity. There's a saying that a successful business has been in business for at least five years or longer. You want to be a part of a business that has a good track record and that pays their employees. True story, I worked for a company with over 60 employees, and the owner failed month after month to pay his 60-plus employees on time.

3. <u>How did they get started?</u> Are they a mom and pop business that grew into a large business, or a company that bought out several businesses? Mom and pop success stories are awesome because they value people, their local community, and may be a bit more forgiving toward a person with a past. Businesses that tend to absorb other businesses can present potential issues with loyalty, employee appreciation, and advancement within the company. This does not mean

a company that buys out businesses would not be a company to work for, but do your research to determine if that company would meet your needs in the long run.

4. <u>What is the company known for?</u> What is the company's vision, and do you believe in it? How has the company vision impacted your community? The reason this is important is because you, as an employee, are investing your time and talent into that business; and therefore, the impact that company has in your community impacts you as well.

If you focus on money, you'll make some for a while, but if you focus on the vision of a business, you will find opportunities for promotion, which will lead to making even more money.

It Is What It Is

As I mentioned in the introduction, I'm an African-American male, a two-time felon, college dropout, born and raised in the city of Cleveland. I have all the ingredients to fail at landing a job and being successful in life, if I allowed it. I admit, after going from temp job to temp job, my confidence, motivation, and esteem were depleting fast. I wanted hiring managers to feel sorry for me or just to hook a brother up with a permanent position, because I lacked the confidence and focus when I was on my temporary work assignments. I lacked confidence because of my prior offenses, not the job assignments. Once I realized that the word FELON was not stamped on my forehead when owners and hiring managers looked at me, my attitude toward myself and how I approached positions I wanted to take on changed. Instead of telling people that I was a convicted felon, I would say that I was a former felon or ex-offender. My point is I'm no longer that guy. It's a thing of the past. What you say or think of yourself today is how employers will think of you as well.

See, companies are looking to hire people that will make their business better and more successful. So I had to look beyond my past faults and find what I had to offer a company. I began to see that I'm resourceful, that I'm not shy around people, I enjoy facing challenges, and solving problems. Once I discovered these values about myself, I began speaking to myself in the mirror, affirming who I am, not what I was. As corny as that may seem, it boosted my confidence. I have even used the mirror to do a mock interview. I would ask myself questions and pay close attention to how I answered the questions while standing in front of the mirror, because deep down I knew that I would be a very good asset to the company to which I was applying. If you're having a hard time getting employed, it may not be due to your past, it may be due to how you see yourself now. When you walk into that company or business to fill out an employment application, walk in with your head up, with a pleasant look on your face, looking the person in the eyes when asking for an application. And don't forget to say please and thank you; it really goes a long way. You want to do this during your job interview as well: head up, look them in the eyes, and a firm handshake, along with please and thank you.

Employers are looking for someone they believe will be reliable, dependable, and competent to get the job done. How you present yourself tells them everything they need to know. If you don't feel that you are reliable, dependable, or competent, start right where you are by practicing on your family and friends. Show your friends and family that you can be trusted, and your future employer will see it, too. Also while you're practicing, practice saying please and thank you, along with looking your friends and family in the eyes when speaking to them. Practice doesn't make you perfect, but it does build more confidence.

Reliable Transportation

I know what you may be thinking. Public transportation such the bus, train, taxi, or even Uber is reliable transportation as long it does not break down, right? Wrong. Borrowing your family member's car or using public transportation is not reliable transportation because it is not your personal transportation. The hiring manager may not ask this question depending on where you live, like New York City or other metropolitan areas. If they do, what they want to know is if you have you own vehicle; is it in working mechanical order, with current tags and registration; and if you have auto insurance and a valid driver's license. The reason they are asking about reliable transportation is that the hiring manager may require you to work a shift or travel beyond the limits of public transportation. Before they hire you, the hiring manager wants to be certain that you will not be tardy, constantly late, or absent because your family member was not able to drop you off or the bus stopped running after a certain hour of the night or early morning.

If you are in the process of getting your vehicle repaired or replaced, be honest about it. Don't explain your life story about how you are trying to get a car or you're working on getting your vehicle fixed. Instead, let them know, "My vehicle is currently not running, but with this position, I would be able to generate the income or money needed to make the necessary repairs." And if you do not own a car and your plan is to get one, tell them, "I currently do not own a vehicle, but I have made arrangements to make sure I'm on time every day for work until I'm able to get my own vehicle." These sample statements tell the hiring manager that you are responsible and that you were planning ahead and anticipating the positions you are applying for. Hiring managers like that. At the end of the day, the hiring manager will decide whether to hire you or not, based on your vehicle situation. If the hiring manager decides to hire you, they now can determine what shift and hours they will allow you to work until you get your vehicle running. Not having a vehicle may possibly restrict a position or your growth potential.

Secondly, the reason hiring managers may ask the question, "Do you have reliable transportation?" is to see how responsible you are. Do you a valid driver's license? If you do not have a valid license, figure out what needs to be done to get one or have it reinstated. In the meantime, be sure to get a state I.D. if you do not drive or have never applied for a driver's license. Not having a driver's license does not mean they will not hire you. However, not having a driver's license can limit you on what position you could get hired for. Regardless, make sure you have current, valid identification. Hiring managers may request a copy of your I.D. to verify that the information on your application is up-to-date and that your I.D. is not expired, fake, or that you do not have warrants out for your arrest.

Finally, even though the hiring manager may not ask if you have proof of insurance, please make sure your vehicle is insured. There is nothing like getting fired because you let your insurance lapse, especially if you use your vehicle for work.

www.LiveDailey.com

www.ingramcontent.com/pod-product-compliance
Lightning Source LLC
Chambersburg PA
CBHW070330190526
45169CB00005B/1830